THE GENE
GOLDEN PATH

GENIUS
A guide to your Activation Sequence

GENE KEYS

This edition published in Great Britain and USA 2020
by Gene Keys Publishing Ltd
13 Freeland Park, Wareham Road, Poole BH16 6FA

Richard Rudd

THE GENE KEYS GOLDEN PATH
GENIUS
A guide to your Activation Sequence

Print edition ISBN 978-1-9996710-0-6
Kindle edition ISBN 978-1-8380487-0-9

The content in this book is purely inspirational which you may choose to use on a personal journey of investigation and exploration. This should not be entered into lightly. It is to be used with the understanding that neither the publisher nor author is engaged to render any type of psychological or other professional advice in any way, shape or form. The content of the course is the sole expression and opinion of its author, and not necessarily that of the publisher. No warranties or guarantees are expressed or implied. The publishers take no responsibility for how you use the content.

genekeys.com

CONTENTS

ABOUT THE AUTHOR

Richard Rudd is an international teacher, writer and award-winning poet. His mystical journey began early in life when he experienced a life changing state of spiritual illumination over 3 days and nights in his twenties. This catalysed an extensive worldwide spiritual search. All his studies became synthesised in 2002 when he began to write and receive the Gene Keys – a vast synthesis exploring the miraculous possibilities inherent in human DNA. It took seven years to write the book as well as understand and embody its teachings. Today Richard continues to study and teach the profound lessons contained in the Gene Keys.

FOREWORD

You are about to begin a beautiful journey into the Purpose of your life. Everyone would like to know why they have come here. This question is as old as the hills. But, as you will discover, the Purpose of your life is not so much about what you are here to do as how you are to do it. What you are here to do is of secondary importance. Our primary purpose is to live well, to live with passion, to learn from our mistakes and to continually expand beyond the parameters set by our minds or the minds of others.

A life in which we make mistakes and take full responsibility for those mistakes, without recourse to blame, is in some ways even more admirable than a life of impeccable morality. Our very human nature is to grow. So the purpose of your life is not a fixed mark. It is an ever-changing alignment to the core of your humanity, to your ability to forgive yourself and others and to keep the fires of your enthusiasm burning ever brightly.

I hope that your journey into this wisdom brings these insights and gifts into your life. I wrote this book so that I could be there with you in some form as you navigate the Gene Keys and the mysteries of your Hologenetic Profile.

The book is designed to go with Part 1 of the online Golden Path Program. I strongly encourage you therefore to use it in conjunction with the program, which also consists of audios, videos and practical guidance in a step-by-step form. The real beauty of the Golden Path is that it need not be overwhelming, but you can pace yourself as you travel this wonderful contemplative journey into the Gene Keys.

Finally, I would like to wish you good fortune as you explore this material. The essence of the Gene Keys is the transformation of the suffering of our past into the Gifts of the future, and therefore that is our greatest challenge as a species. Thank you for having the courage to take this pioneering step and may it reward you in a myriad of marvellous and unexpected ways.

Richard Rudd

1. INTRODUCTION

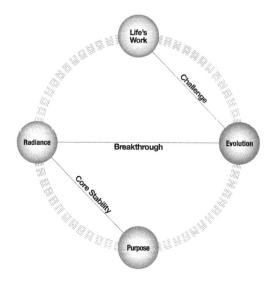

A CONTEMPORARY I CHING

THE FIRE EYE

Deep inside the arc of your being there is an eye. This eye was born when you were born, and it will die when you die. This is the Fire Eye. When you see the world through this eye, you see a world of adventure, of excitement, of passion. When you see through the Fire Eye, everything is vibrant and changing and bursting with potential – the very air around you crackles with the electricity of your longing. Through the Fire Eye, you live in the unpredictable and ever-changing landscape of dreams – one moment you are wandering carefree through the green valleys of comfort, and the next you are staggering hopelessly through the parched deserts of desire.

It is the Fire Eye inside you that has led you here. It is the seeker inside you, the inquirer, the believer, the knower. The Fire Eye leads you on a dance through life as you leap from one experience to another. It lures you across continents and carries you over the threshold of every relationship in your life.

The Fire Eye never ceases to dream of what once was, or of what may one day become. When you look out at life through the Fire Eye, you wonder about the purpose of your life. You may feel you could be doing more. You know you have so much to give but you don't yet know how to give it. You feel a restless longing to accomplish something, to fulfil your highest destiny.

The Fire Eye dreams large dreams. As the turbine that drives all human genius, the Fire Eye knows that anything in life is possible. It has already accomplished so much in our world. It is the Fire Eye that builds the great civilisations and puts men on the moon.

It is the Fire Eye that drives our human evolution. Those whose lives have unfolded through the Fire Eye have become our great heroes and heroines – those great statesmen, warriors, explorers, inventors and geniuses whose lives remain forever enshrined in our history.

As the energy of eternal youth inside you – the Fire Eye is wonderfully dynamic, endlessly hungry and always, always filled with hope. But for all its fertile vitality and raw power, the Fire Eye has a flaw. It is self-obsessed.

The Fire Eye cannot see beyond its own need for satiation. Like a wild dog chasing its own tail, it does not know how to rest. No matter how great are its achievements in the world; the Fire Eye is not capable of finding inner peace.

THE WATER EYE

Deep inside the arc of your being there is another eye. This eye was present before you were born and it will remain after you die. This is the Water Eye. When you see the world through this eye, you see only that which is before you. When you see through the Water Eye, your primary awareness rests with your breath, your body and its gentle rhythms, and with the movement of life all around you. When you see through the Water Eye, all of life sees with you, and all of life comes towards you. Through the lens of the Water Eye, all is still, all is quiet and all is fathomless.

Perhaps it is the Water Eye that has led you here. If you are here because you do not know, then you may be in for a gentle surprise.

The Water Eye has no interest in achievement or knowledge or dreams. It has no interest in purpose or fulfilment or change. The Water Eye has no interest in human experience.

Rare is the human being who can give their life over to the Water Eye. It is the subtlest of the subtle. It is the softest, most paradoxical, most mysterious presence inside you. The Water Eye is a power without force, without emotion, without warmth. If you allow the lens of the Water Eye to open inside your being, you will begin to view your life and the world in a completely new way.

In the outer world, the Water Eye has built nothing. There is nothing impressive about it. It passes unnoticed. Those whose lives have unfolded through the Water Eye have generally been misunderstood and misrepresented. They did not discover it on purpose for it cannot be chased or hunted or sought.

Of all the mysteries in the universe, the Water Eye alone brings inner peace. But for all its allure and wonder, nothing you do in life will lead to its opening. The Water Eye responds to one thing and one thing alone.

It responds to the one who yields.

THE GENE KEYS AND THE GOLDEN PATH

Putting The Fire Beneath The Water

If you have been drawn to the Gene Keys, then you may already know that it is based upon the ancient code of the Chinese I Ching – the Book of Changes. This deeply mysterious book continues to circle the world in many diverse forms. Its most common use is as an oracle – a tool to give subtle guidance in any given life situation. In essence, the I Ching is designed to attune you to the presence of that subtlest inner wisdom – the Water Eye within you.

The ancient Chinese had their own words for the Fire Eye and the Water Eye. They called them the Hsin and the Yi respectively. When used over time, the correct use of the I Ching is a spiritual path in itself.

It will guide you to listen to your innate, silent, intuitive wisdom - your 'Yi' (the Water Eye) above and beyond your human desires and longings - your 'Hsin' (the Fire Eye). Unfortunately, our modern global lifestyle is so strongly developed around the Fire Eye, that even the I Ching has now mostly become another toy for that restless longing inside us. We no longer realise the level of commitment that the I Ching requires of its students. Like most sacred and magical texts, it has now been taken far away from its original context, and its true secrets lie for the most part lost to modern humans.

This is where the Gene Keys come into play. The Gene Keys are a contemporary adaptation of the I Ching and the Golden Path provides a structured and disciplined means of contemplation on the teachings themselves. The Golden Path allows you to take the Gene Keys deeply into your daily life. It is designed to be contemplated over a period of time so that you can absorb its insights and experience its transformational power.

The advantage of this form is that you do not have to change very much externally in your life. You adjust the teachings to your daily rhythms, rather than the other way around. As your contemplation deepens over time, the living wisdom within you begins to awaken at a new level, leading to unexpected changes and new vistas opening up before you. This is a process referred to as Self Illumination.

As you contemplate your Golden Path it will act as a reminder to yield to life. It will consistently nudge you to listen to the subtle wisdom of the Water Eye within, and it will compassionately assist you to transform the many challenges that come from listening only to the Fire Eye – your emotions and desires. The potential of the Golden Path is to remind you of the secret of alchemy – to put the fire beneath the water.

This is a gradual process of coming into equilibrium, in which many hidden gifts inside you may come to the surface. Ultimately the Golden Path is a rich inner voyage into the deep mystery of the Self. Because it is a mystery, there is no way of predicting what may occur in your life as a result of following this path. The only way to find out is to step forward bravely, trusting in the inner light that already lies inside you.

THE GENE KEYS GOLDEN PATH

The following section provides important background information that you will need before you begin to work with the three sequences that comprise the Gene Keys Golden Path. It begins by introducing the tools and terminology for your contemplation and shows you how to use them. It also helps to clarify the central technique of contemplation as well as offering an overall spiritual perspective as to how best approach the Gene Keys themselves.

When you first come to the Gene Keys you will discover that there are many different elements and processes that underpin this knowledge. We will explore these in Part 2 of this introduction, but in essence it can all be brought down to three essential elements:

1. The Gene Keys – your map

2. The Hologenetic Profile – your compass

3. The Golden Path – your journey

To begin this journey you will need to have a copy of the Gene Keys book as well as a copy of your Hologenetic Profile.

YOUR HOLOGENETIC PROFILE

Your Hologenetic Profile is a personalised map of the unique inner contours of your consciousness. The Golden Path describes a transformational route through this map. This is your own path through the mystery of the Gene Keys, and as you follow it, it may bring about many changes in your life. You can easily obtain a free copy of your individual Hologenetic Profile from the Gene Keys website.

Derived from a system known as Human Design, your Hologenetic Profile is calculated from the time, date and place of your birth. It pinpoints the specific positions of the sun and planets at the precise moment of your birth and places them within a wheel or mandala known as the I Ching Wheel. The I Ching Wheel is an ancient means of using the 64 hexagrams of the I Ching in a circle rather than in their more traditional form as a grid.

Your Hologenetic Profile translates a single moment of imprinting, your birth, into a series of coordinates in the space-time continuum. These coordinates are then mapped onto their 64 corresponding codons within your DNA. We can then use the Gene Keys to decipher the archetypal meaning of these numbers. Even though it may sound complex, it is in fact very logical and very simple. Understandably, some may question the connection between the positions of planets and the genesis of human DNA. However, when you understand the universe in which we live as holographic, then we see that all patterns within space-time are linked through a vast hyper-dimensional matrix.

Therefore the patterns in the heavens always have a direct correspondence to emergent life. It is not that one influences the other, but that one is literally entangled with the other at a quantum level.

Your Hologenetic profile helps you to see the nature of the forces that underpin your destiny. It is 'hologenetic' because everything within your profile is connected to everything else, just as all the DNA within your body operates as a single unified information field. When you begin to contemplate the specific Gene Keys in your Profile, you therefore activate the corresponding patterns within your physical body. This is what makes working with your Profile so powerful.

THE ELEMENTS OF YOUR HOLOGENETIC PROFILE

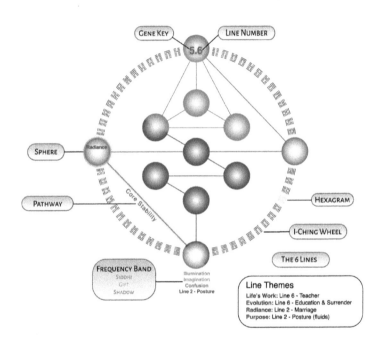

THE TECHNIQUE - CONTEMPLATION

THE GOLDEN PATH AND THE ART OF CONTEMPLATION

The central technique that underpins the entire spectrum of the Gene Keys teachings is contemplation. It is an important term to clarify as it already carries different meanings within different languages and cultures. In the introduction to the Gene Keys book, the three classic paths to truth are outlined. They are called meditation, concentration and contemplation. Since contemplation is a blend of the other two it is important to fully understand their relationship, and you are invited to suspend any previous understanding you may have concerning these words.

MEDITATION

When we refer here to meditation, we are referring to more than just a technique. Meditation is a fundamental path leading towards enlightened spiritual understanding. Meditation is the great feminine or 'yin' path and is also known is some cultures as the 'left hand' path. Meditation is primarily involved with the 'right brain' approach to life, which is holistic rather than reductionist. Meditation is well exemplified in the Buddhist tradition by the word 'vipassana' which can be translated as deep-seeing. This kind of meditation is based on watching, waiting, listening, witnessing and allowing. This also correlates with the ancient spirit of 'tantra', which is based upon an all-embracing view of the universe.

From the perspective of the Gene Keys, meditation is a path in which you simply go along with whatever is emerging in your life. You do not in any way resist your nature. This is beautifully caught by the Advaita Vedanta tradition, in which everything is viewed as perfect the way it is.

Even if you forget, it's still perfect. If you are angry, impatient, mean or any other negative state, it is part of the emerging perfection of the totality. To use the simple metaphor of life as a river, in meditation your awareness is just sitting quietly beside the river.

You just sit there watching life go by, and slowly, over time, as you watch life without judgement (or even with judgement) an inner core begins to become aware of itself inside you. As this core emerges you are able to let go even more of trying to control things and follow life. This is the path of effortlessness and deep trust.

CONCENTRATION

Concentration lies at the opposite end of the spectrum from meditation. Concentration is the Yang path or the right hand path, the path of effort. The right hand path is rooted in the left hemisphere of the brain – the logical brain that sees consciousness as a process of questing that can be fulfilled in stages over time. Concentration correlates to yoga, in the widest use of the word. Yoga begins with the premise that somehow you've fallen out of union. So you take on this yoga and you begin to work to bring yourself back to union. You set off on a journey to recover your true nature.

Effort is needed in the path of concentration. In the West it has always been a strong path – exemplified in the path of prayer - the path of heading back towards God. An Eastern example of this approach is Zen. In Zen, especially the Rinzai version of Zen, you sit and concentrate your mind and your full being on a koan, a paradox. Finally through that concentration, which may take years and years of effort, you break through and see the true nature of reality.

There are many types of yoga - karma yoga, bhakti yoga, mantra yoga - and they all move towards the same truth

– they are all efforts moving towards truth. This is what is meant by concentration.

CONTEMPLATION

Contemplation is the no-hand path. It borrows elements from both meditation and concentration. In some respects contemplation is a forgotten path. Of all the world teachings, the one most related to the essence of contemplation is the Tao. Because it is less easy to define than meditation and concentration, it sometimes seems a more nebulous path, and this is its one disadvantage.

However, when it is correctly understood and practised, it is a less extreme path than the other two and is particularly suited to our practical, everyday lives.

Contemplation uses the sustained pressure of concentration in order to create the conditions for a breakthrough to occur. However, contemplation is a gentler approach than concentration and it doesn't push too hard in any direction. It presupposes that breakthrough can only occur in a state of relaxation and play. There is a well-known story about the Buddha overhearing a musician. The man said that if you tighten the string of your instrument too far, it will snap, but if you have it too slack it will not play music. Out of this insight the 'Middle Way' was born. Like the Middle Way, contemplation is a dance with the opposites. It uses sustained pressure in a playful way and this also makes it a less formal path than concentration or meditation.

In the introduction to the Gene Keys, there is a metaphor for the spirit of contemplation. It describes a small ring case such as you might find at an expensive jewellers. The case is covered in sumptuous velvet, and somewhere inside a thing of mysterious beauty lies hidden. Amid the countless folds of velvet is a tiny hidden catch. You take the case in your hands and you roll it gently through your fingers. You don't know what you are looking for but you just enjoy the feel of the soft velvet while you allow your fingers to explore the case. At a certain point, you find the hidden catch and all of a sudden the case springs open to reveal the treasure. Contemplation is such a search. It is not an intense search, rather it is a playful appreciation of mystery, content to enjoy the journey itself as much as the breakthroughs along the way.

The key in contemplation is to have an object to Contemplate. You need an object with enough dimensions to sustain your practise. This is what the Gene Keys are designed for.

To some, contemplation may sound like a mental word, and at one level it is. We do use our minds to consider the mysteries of the inner dimensions. But we also use other aspects of our being at the same time. Contemplation is a trinary path. We contemplate mentally, emotionally and physically.

As you learn more about the different stages and sequences of the Golden Path you will see how these three levels of contemplation are interwoven.

MODES OF CONTEMPLATION

1. Spheres And Pathways

When you look at your Hologenetic Profile you will see that it is made up of a grid of circles or spheres, which are in turn connected by a series of pathways and arrows. Some people might notice a similarity here between the ancient teachings of the Jewish Kabbalah. As a new synthesis, the Gene Keys stands on the shoulders of many of the great systems of the past, and by combining them it seeks to present an even deeper view of reality.

Each of the 11 spheres of your Profile represents an aspect of your life on which you may contemplate. As you place your awareness on a particular sphere and its corresponding Gene Key, you will be opening up the potential for insight and transformation to occur in that realm. For example, as you contemplate the sphere of your Life's Work, you may begin to understand aspects of your past in a new light. At the same time you may also begin to realise that you have a far greater potential for a new future than you have allowed yourself to believe. This change in the frequency of your beliefs is what makes the Gene Keys so powerful.

There are also eleven pathways that link the eleven spheres together in what appears to be a linear flow. These pathways represent the dynamic processes that underpin your destiny. At low levels of frequency, the inner light or life force inside you becomes choked in these channels and our natural evolution becomes stalled.

As your contemplation on each sphere deepens, you can experience striking periods of transformation or breakthrough as this inner light begins to flow once again through your life. This process of self-illumination takes time and requires sustained contemplation and patience. As your frequency becomes raised, you also begin to see how each sphere and pathway is part of a holographic whole.

For example, as you experience a shift in your mental beliefs, so you will see this reflected in your physical body and in your relationships.

MODES OF CONTEMPLATION

2. Gene Keys And The 6 Lines

The 64 Gene Keys themselves are the programming language of inner consciousness. As you contemplate your own Gene Keys and even those that do not appear in your own Profile, you are directly imbibing the universal truth at the heart of these teachings. In addition to this, the story of each Gene Key

15

is focussed through one of 6 possible lenses known as the 6 lines. The revelation of the 6 lines comes directly from the mathematical structure of the I Ching and its 64 Hexagrams. A hexagram is a symbol made up of 6 lines and each line adds a certain colour to the Gene Key. If you imagine that each Gene Key is like an individual melody in music, then the 6 lines would be like 6 different keys that those melodies could be played in. The same melody would sound very different in each key, so the importance of understanding the line together with the Gene Key cannot be underestimated.

As you learn to understand the timbre of each line, you will find it easier to apply them to the 64 Gene Keys. This means that there are 6 x 64 permutations of the Gene Keys, making 384 fascinating stories. The inclusion of the 6 lines is one of the things that make contemplating the Gene Keys so special.

You have to release the power of your imagination coupled with your intuition as it works through the formula of the 6 lines. This can lead to surprising and uplifting insights. Contemplation on the Gene Keys and the 6 lines is an empowering process as it is something you learn to do yourself. It allows you a certain freedom to rove within the living text and explore its hidden capacities for awakening those secrets that lie hidden within.

THE VOYAGE - TREADING THE GOLDEN PATH

The Golden Path is a path into the deep mystery. It is a path of soul, in which your daily living becomes your greatest muse. It is a path of enrichment, which at the same time trains a fierce eye upon the way you are living. It asks you to contemplate some profound and sometimes painful questions. As you tread the Golden Path, you will take a deep dive into three primary questions:

1. What is your purpose in life?

2. How fulfilling are your relationships?

3. How integrated are you into your community?

When human beings are in harmony with creation, these three questions simply do not exist. In essence, the Golden Path describes the organic flow of life when it follows natural rhythms without resistance. There may have been times in human history when this was the case, but our modern world is very clearly not one of these times. This is the purpose of the Gene Keys – to assist individuals, relationships and communities in realigning their lives back into a wider harmony with creation itself.

In the original I Ching, the most common translation of the 10th Hexagram is the word 'Treading'. In the Gene Keys, its equivalent, the 10th Gene Key, is the Gift of Naturalness. As we tread the paths of our lives, so we write our destinies. The further we move from our essential nature, the more we and those around us suffer. And this suffering is vital to us. It keeps reminding us of the simplest path, the path of least resistance, the path that is naturally ours. It has been said that the hardest and the easiest thing in the world is simply to be yourself.

The Buddha referred to this Golden Path as the Middle Way – the natural curve and slide of our inner evolution as it manifests in the outer world.

As we unravel the thread of our true destiny, so our natural path begins to shine before us and open beneath us. It becomes illuminated by our inner awareness, and in this sense, our lives become golden. Treading the Golden Path is a gesture of deep faith in ourselves. It takes courage and a great deal of not-knowing.

THE STRUCTURE OF DESTINY

Human destiny unravels according to its own timing and structure. The Golden Path provides a structure that allows you to contemplate the Gene Keys in a personalised way, with specific Gene Keys relating to certain areas of your life. This is an inner voyage you will take over a period of time.

The Golden Path has three archetypal stages:

Part 1. Discovering your Purpose - Activation Sequence

Part 2. Opening your Heart – Venus Sequence

Part 3. Releasing your Prosperity – Pearl Sequence

Each of these three stages relates to the three questions above concerning purpose, relationships and community, and even though they may seem different from each other, you may well discover for yourself how deeply interconnected they are.

No matter which phase of your life you are currently travelling through, you will see that the whole of your life is really a journey into purpose, love and prosperity. The intricate tapestry of your destiny depends on the art you bring to the actual process of daily living. As you take the journey through these three stages of the Golden Path, you will have the wonderful opportunity to grasp something of the structure of your own destiny, woven as it is into the fabric of your living DNA.

APPLYING THE GENE KEYS TO YOUR LIFE

The Magic Of Sequences

If you decide to tread the Golden Path through the Gene Keys, you are recommended to begin at the natural beginning, which is with the Activation Sequence and your four Prime Gifts. The magic of the Golden Path is that it provides you with a sequential structure to contemplate that unravels over time.

All of life and evolution follows natural sequences. However, the sequences of the Golden Path are not paths of development that change who you are. They are an unravelling of your highest essence that lies hidden within. Therefore when you travel these sequences, it is as though you are unpicking the tapestry of your life in reverse. You must check each stitch of the fabric and discard those knots and slips that have caused your life to take you into difficulties. Then as you rewire your own genetic patterns, you will be recreating your entire life from a clean slate.

Following your sequences takes time. You are asked to make a deep contemplation of your beliefs, your behaviour, your thought-life and the nature of your desires and dreams. The sequences will reveal to you anything that is out of alignment with the whole, and you will discard those parts of yourself that do not serve a higher purpose. This is the magic of the sequences at work - they are practical and they are transformational.

19

STAGE 1. THE ACTIVATION SEQUENCE

Grounding On The Physical Plane

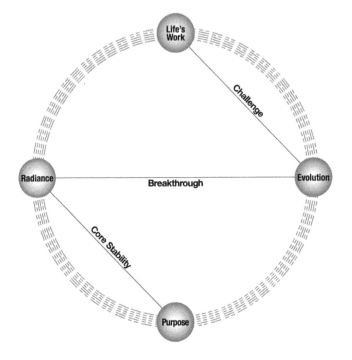

The Activation Sequence is the simplest of the 3 sequences that comprise the Golden Path. It serves a powerful purpose in orienting you physically into your body, into the centre of your inner world. It is a celebration of the beauty and dignity of your aloneness. As you contemplate the Gene Keys of your 4 Prime Gifts and their inner dynamics, you engage the activation sequence within you, which lays the foundation for a breakthrough in your life.

As you continue working with the Gene Keys through the other sequences, these breakthroughs will be ongoing. For this reason the Activation Sequence sets the foundation for your journey of transformation.

STAGE 2. THE VENUS SEQUENCE

Navigating The Emotional Realm

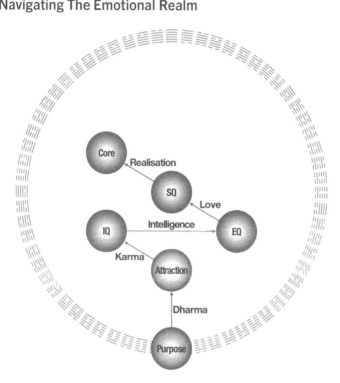

As the longest and most complex of the 3 sequences you will contemplate along the Golden Path, the Venus Sequence represents the core of these teachings. It is a journey into the heart and the wounding that we all carry around our hearts. The Venus Sequence reorients you in your life at an emotional level, exploring genetic themes of holding and release woven from the ancestral DNA you inherited at birth.

As you contemplate your Venus Sequence and its Gene Keys, you bring the transformation into your relationships through an increased awareness of the patterns that prevent you from living consistently with an open heart.

STAGE 3. THE PEARL SEQUENCE
Clarifying Vision On The Mental Plane

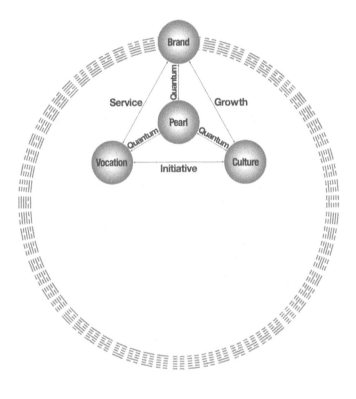

When you arrive at the Pearl Sequence, you may begin to view many aspects of your life in a new light. As you spend time activating the higher frequencies of the Gene Keys inside you, a new vision of your life begins to dawn. This vision comes as a natural unfolding once your emotional patterns are understood and accepted. Once you begin to relate clearly and cleanly with others, the codes of your higher purpose begin to attract new opportunities towards you. The Pearl Sequence assists you in clarifying exactly how you are best designed to serve the whole. The Pearl shows you how your unique talents can best be used to ensure you become truly prosperous at all levels.

Each of the three sequences of the Golden Path are part of an unfolding mystery that will take you on a journey of transformation into your everyday life. Even though each sequence appears separate and moves within time, they are in fact all interconnected. The magic of these linear sequences is that they paradoxically intensify your experience of the present moment.

WORKING AND PLAYING WITH THE GENE KEYS

There are many ways of using the Gene Keys in your life. They are an invitation to your own imagination. The Golden Path is simply one of these many ways, and if understood correctly, it offers one of the steepest expansion curves you may ever have encountered in your life. The time you give to this process may well propel you into a whole new phase in your life. Therefore the Golden Path is a path to tread lightly but not to take lightly. It has the capacity to pull you sharply back into your own centre, into the steep, untrespassed sanctity of your aloneness.

The central path of the Gene Keys is one of contemplation. You imbibe the truths of the Keys inside yourself over a sustained period of time. You play with the Gene Keys, offering them up to the power of your imagination, until your body begins to inwardly glow with a new lightness. The Gene Keys are about igniting the light that lies dormant within your own core. Indeed, they are a contemplation on light itself. The secret lies in sustained contemplation. In this sense, contemplation is a lifelong endeavour. This doesn't mean you have to contemplate the Gene Keys for the rest of your life, but that at a certain point you will no longer need them and they will fall away naturally as you begin to embody the truth of their wisdom in your daily life.

INDIVIDUATION - THE PURPOSE OF THE JOURNEY

As was stated earlier, the Golden Path is about bringing a
higher harmony back into our lives. It is about being natural.
It is about seeing life through the Water Eye - that part of us
that can always sense and follow the path of least resistance
in life. The final goal of the Golden Path is to bring you to
a state known as 'individuation'. Individuation refers to a
process whereby the many different aspects of your life - your
dreams, your relationships, your health, your finances, your
spirituality - are brought together into an integrated harmony.

An individuated human being is a person whose inner life
is in exact harmony with their outer life. In such a person,
everything has become simplified. The power of your
aloneness is the font of your strength, but it in no way isolates
you from your community. On the contrary, your aloneness
serves to strengthen your bonds within your community. In
an individuated being, many emotional states are naturally
processed and transmuted internally, causing far less friction,
confusion or energy loss in the environment.

This also brings far more ease and simplicity into all your
relationships. The more individuated you become, the more
energy efficient you become. At the same time, individuation
does not mean you will become more 'spiritual'. It retains
full involvement of our passions and those difficult states
we often refer to as our Shadows. The difference between an
individuated human being and a conditioned human being
is that the former lives in a state of self-forgiveness.

Individuation should be understood as different from any
so-called spiritual state. It is not the same as enlightenment
or realisation. Rather it is a prerequisite for such states.
Individuation speaks of an inner maturity in which the
hungry search for spiritual truth has settled down inside us,
bringing our whole system into a profound sense of balance

and ease. When we come into a state of individuation our spirituality has become internalised. We are naturally inclined to speak less about our insight and to maintain appropriate boundaries around ourselves emotionally and psychologically.

At the same time, we find that the ordinary world around us is welcoming and fruitful and we meet it with a refreshing sense of openness.

The individuated human being rarely separates him or herself from the marketplace but is content to move among the world as an ordinary person. Individuation is a powerful and humble place to arrive at in your life. It may not appear exciting to the externally hungry mind, but it conveys the secret weight of the patience and calm that you have anchored deep into your DNA. To be individuated is to court the subtle and the invisible and at the same time it is to shine out with the light of your humanity.

To tread the Golden Path through the Gene Keys is a grand adventure. It is an ancient adventure clothed in a contemporary form. While its potential is life changing, much depends upon you the voyager. You are invited to bring your full imaginative self into the process. It is your journey into your life, and the more honest and aware you can be with yourself, the more profound your self-illumination will be.

2. YOUR ACTIVATION SEQUENCE

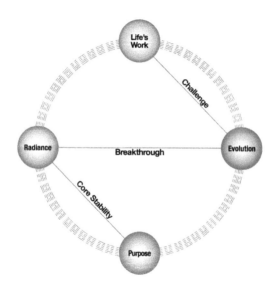

YOUR ACTIVATION SEQUENCE
DISCOVERING YOUR GENIUS

THE FOUR PRIME GIFTS

Before the Gene Keys came into being, I was a student of a system known as the Human Design System. Indeed, part of the revelation of the Gene Keys rests on the foundation of Human Design. In Human Design, the birth chart contains these same four coordinates referred to as your four Prime Gifts. In Human Design they are referred to as an 'incarnation cross' and they denote over seventy percent of your being. As I studied Human Design, I became fascinated by these 4 coordinates. I entered into a profound contemplation of them over a period of years. Finally one day, the light dawned inside me. These were not simply a locked set of parameters that described an individual as a set of characteristics. This was a code, and inside the code hides a secret, and the secret could only be unlocked in a sequence, just like the combination lock of a vault.

Like most people I love a mystery. But I have also learned something over the years. It is that a mystery can be unlocked, but never solved. A true mystery, like life itself, is not for us to understand with our logical mind. Puzzles can be solved, but never a true mystery. You are such a mystery. There are many systems that claim to solve the mystery that is you. They may attempt to pigeonhole us into categories and behaviours and types, but no human being can be broken down into parts in this way. We are meant to be a mystery. Knowing this, you are free to explore consciousness in an unfettered way. You will not have to learn any new information. Contemplation is not about learning. It is about revealing, unzipping, unfurling. There are answers, but there is no definitive answer.

Your four Prime Gifts are living archetypes that float within this mystery. They are imprinted codes hanging in the hologram of space-time. Like the 64 hexagrams of the original I Ching, the 64 Gene Keys are portals into the dynamic nexus of all existence – change. Your Prime Gifts are the seeds of your potential transformation.

They may just seem to be words on a page, but when the light of your contemplation is consistently shined upon them, they actually affect you. They begin to reprogram the way you see yourself, the way you sit within your body, the way you respond to life.

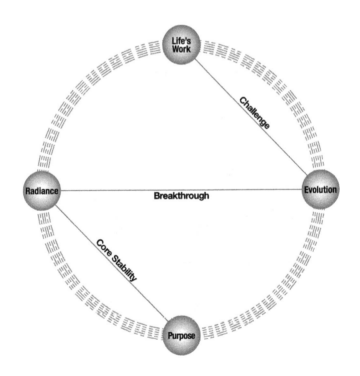

Your Activation Sequence represents the beginning of a voyage into the living matrix of the Gene Keys. It is the practical means of unlocking the higher purpose hidden in your DNA. These 4 Prime Gifts are the pillars of your genius, so as you contemplate them, you should understand that they encode the living fabric of your destiny. Until you truly understand each one of these four Gene Keys – your Life's Work, your Evolution, your Radiance and your Purpose, then some part of your destiny will still remain dormant.

In the Golden Path, the sequence is always the key. In genetics, everything inside us is laid down in a sequence and everything is unlocked in a sequence. All physical change comes about because somewhere inside us a sequence has been activated. For cellular change to take place, the RNA unzips the DNA by running down a string of nucleotides in a sequence. All the processes of life work in this same way. Evolution itself is a code that spontaneously unlocks itself in sequences. It is both comforting and scintillating to think that all the mysteries of life lie locked away behind these hidden codes. Science unlocks the physical mysteries, but contemplation unlocks the spiritual mysteries. Within the burgeoning revelation of the Gene Keys, everything begins here with your Activation Sequence.

RELEVANT TERMINOLOGY FOR CONTEMPLATION

Throughout this book and your journey with the Golden Path you are swimming within a rich field of high frequency terminology. This is one of the things that makes working with your Profile so powerful. As you contemplate and turn these words over inside yourself they can help you to gain clarity and insight. At times within the text you will come across new terms. Most of these terms are defined in the Glossary of Personal Empowerment at the back of the Gene Keys book (2nd edition onwards), but many of them are also included here and some are new. Instead of putting these terms in a glossary at the back of this book (which you might forget to read), I have included them here at the beginning. Each term carries an empowerment, so they can be rewarding to read and contemplate. Before moving on, you are advised to read through these definitions and let them settle inside your awareness. This will be an important aspect of your ongoing contemplative practise with the Gene Keys.

Activation Sequence — The Activation Sequence is the primary genetic sequence in your Hologenetic Profile. The Activation Sequence describes a series of three leaps in awareness that unfold in your life as you activate the higher purpose within your DNA. These inner realisations are called your Challenge, your Breakthrough and your Core Stability. Calculated from the position of the sun at the time of your birth, your Activation Sequence pinpoints four specific Gene Keys (known as your Four Prime Gifts) that form the vibratory field of your genius. As its name suggests, your Activation Sequence is a trigger that can catalyse a period of intense transformation in your life.

Awareness — An aspect of consciousness unique to all life forms. In a human being, awareness can be divided into three main layers, although in reality they are all a single awareness — physical awareness, emotional awareness and mental awareness.

At low levels of frequency, human awareness is confined to the human body — physical awareness remains rooted in survival and fear, emotional awareness remains rooted in desire and drama and mental awareness remains rooted in comparison and judgment. As you raise the frequency throughout your being, your awareness becomes more refined and shifts from the local environment to the cosmic. Physical awareness becomes Divine presence, emotional awareness becomes universal love and mental awareness becomes silence and wisdom.

Concentration — One of the three primary paths leading to the higher states of Absorption and Embodiment. Concentration is the left hand path, represented by the ancient science of yoga. It utilises focused effort and willpower to bring about a series of transformations that gradually raise the frequency of your awareness.

Contemplation — One of the three primary paths leading to the higher states of Absorption and Embodiment. Contemplation is the central path, represented by the Tao. It utilises elements of both concentration (effort) and meditation (no effort) to bring about a heightening of your frequency. Contemplation takes place on all three of the lower human planes; there is physical contemplation, emotional contemplation and mental contemplation. Over time, contemplation transforms the physical, astral and mental bodies into their higher frequency counterparts — the causal, buddhic and atmic bodies. Prolonged contemplation on the 64 Gene Keys is one of the quickest and easiest ways to activate the higher frequencies lying latent within your DNA.

Frequency Band — In the Gene Keys Synthesis, the vibratory rate of your aura is mirrored in three frequency 'bands' known as the Shadow, the Gift and the Siddhi. Although there are in fact many layers or bandwidths of frequency, this threefold language makes the Gene Keys simple to understand, contemplate and ultimately embody. The three frequency bands are laid out precisely through the Spectrum of Consciousness – the linguistic map of the 64 Gene Keys and their frequency bands.

Frequency — A means of measuring the vibratory nature of radiant energy such as sound, light or even awareness. The central premise of the Gene Keys Synthesis is that you can alter the frequency of light passing through your DNA, thereby speeding up or slowing down the force of evolution itself. Through deep contemplation on the 64 Gene Keys and their teachings, you can raise the frequency of your DNA and thus change the vibratory frequency of your aura, coming into higher and higher states of harmony with the entire universe.

Gene Key — One of 64 universal attributes of consciousness. Each Gene Key is a multi-dimensional portal into your inner being whose sole purpose is to activate your higher purpose and ultimately allow you to embrace your own Divinity. Your higher purpose is activated through sustained contemplation of the Gene Keys and their frequency bands.

Genius — The innate intelligence of all human beings. True genius (as opposed to intellectual genius) is a spontaneous and unstudied creative uniqueness rooted in unconditional love. Genius is the natural manifestation of a human life when it is allowed to expand without force. Genius is a hallmark of the Gift frequency band where self-forgiveness leads to a progressive opening of your heart, resulting in an explosion of creative energy throughout your being. The higher the frequency of your DNA rises, the greater your urge will be to use your genius in service to the whole. As more and more people join their genius together, the world as we see it today will be transformed.

Gift (Frequency) — The frequency band relating to human genius and open-heartedness. As your awareness enters more fully into the Shadow frequencies, it unlocks latent energy held within your DNA. This energy is released through your physical, astral and mental bodies as light. Physically, this can lead to changes in your body chemistry and increased vitality. Emotionally, it can lead to uplifting feelings, joyousness and a pervading sense of optimism. Mentally, it can lead to insight and great creativity.

The Gift frequency is a process of gradual revelation as your true higher nature (the Siddhi) is unveiled. There are many states and stages within the Gift frequency band and it represents the quantum field where the forces of involution and evolution come together. One of the hallmarks of the Gift frequency is the ability to take full responsibility for one's own karma – that is one's thoughts, feelings, words and actions. At this level of frequency, one no longer identifies as a victim of any perceived external stimulus.

Hexagram — A pictographic binary symbol that forms the basis of the I Ching. The 64 hexagrams of the I Ching are directly analogous to the 64 Gene Keys. Each hexagram is made up of six lines, either broken (yin) or unbroken (yang). The Gene Keys offer a modern interpretation of the 64 hexagrams as they relate to our core genetic structure and to the underlying structure of the universe itself. Each Hexagram or Gene Key is a portal to an encyclopaedia of knowledge and insight about yourself and your place in the universe. Through sustained contemplation on the hexagrams, their structure and interdependence, you can raise the frequency of light moving through your DNA and experience life at a new level of awareness.

I Ching — The original 'prima materia' of the Gene Keys, the I Ching is a sacred Chinese text dating from around the 4th century BC. Many commentaries and versions of the I Ching exist and it is perhaps best known as a popular oracle. The Gene Keys are a natural culmination of all previous incarnations of the I Ching. They ultimately point to the truth that all sacred texts have their source inside us. The same truths intuitively grasped by the ancient sages can now be proven by modern genetics — that the universe is built upon natural codes and these codes can be deciphered and unlocked. The original I Ching was held in the highest esteem as a sacred text with the capacity to mirror living wisdom in every moment. Likewise the Gene Keys point us inwardly to seek the source of our suffering in our Shadows and guide us in transforming that suffering into creativity and freedom.

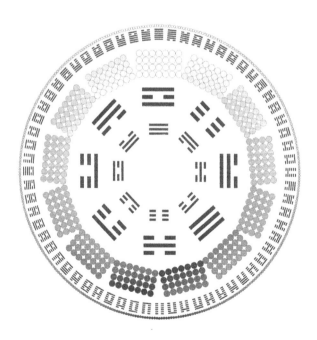

Meditation — One of the three primary paths leading to the higher states of Absorption and Embodiment. Meditation is the right hand path, represented by the ancient science of tantra. The true essence of the meditative path is to simply watch, witness and allow. Through meditation one gradually comes to the realisation that one's true nature dwells in a choice-less awareness. This great revelation may come as a gentle unfolding that raises the frequency of your awareness over time or as a sudden implosion that allows you a permanent experience of your Divine Self — or it may come as both.

Mutation — An unpredictable event that breaks the continuity in any linear sequence, at any level within the universe. In genetic terms, mutations are 'mistakes' made during cell replication. Mutation is the mother of difference, since it creates endless forks in the evolutionary impulse, leading to new and unseen processes. In our everyday lives, mutations also occur all the time. They occur whenever there is a break in the established patterns or rhythms of your life.

It is our fear of mutation that fuels the Shadow frequency field. For example, when you find yourself moving through a period of mutation, you will feel a profound uncertainty about yourself and your life. If you repress or react to this feeling out of fear, you will disturb the processes of good fortune that always accompany mutation. As you learn to surrender to the natural mutative processes in your life, you will unlock the powerful creative gifts inside you and place yourself in alignment with the synchronicity of your true destiny.

Pathway — In your Hologenetic Profile, the dynamic transformational processes that are either held in check by the Shadow frequencies of the Gene Keys or unlocked by their higher frequencies. Each Pathway acts as a conductor of the twin forces of evolution and involution.

Pearl Sequence — The third and final sequence comprising the Golden Path, the Pearl Sequence is the primary genetic sequence for opening up our mental awareness to operate on a higher plane. Constructed from the positions of Mars, Jupiter and the sun at the time of your birth, the Pearl Sequence is a contemplative journey using the Gene Keys whose purpose is to open your mind to a transcendent view of the universe. Such a view allows one to see the inherent simplicity of life and move one's energies and resources into alignment with it. Your individual Pearl Sequence is made up of four specific Gene Keys which have a direct bearing on your ability to be efficient and prosperous in your life. Each of these four Gene Keys shows you a Shadow pattern that prevents you from living a prosperous and liberating life. As your awareness enters into these patterns and unlocks their hidden Gifts, you will discover a resource of untapped genius and creativity. The other great secret of the Pearl Sequence is the power of philanthropy as a world view. The Pearl allows us to find our closest allies and work together in service to our community and a higher goal.

Prime Gifts — Calculated by the time, date and place of your birth, the Prime Gifts are a series of four Gene Keys that relate profoundly to your overall purpose in life.

Known as your Life's Work, your Evolution, your Radiance and your Purpose, the Prime Gifts represent the living field of your genius that was imprinted in your DNA at the point of conception. By understanding and embracing the Shadow aspects of the Gene Keys that correspond to your four Prime Gifts you will activate their higher frequencies and catalyse a mutation to take place deep within your DNA. This process is known as the Activation Sequence. By sustained contemplation on the highest frequencies of your four Prime Gifts you will witness a complete transformation in your life as you unlock the true genius inside you.

Programming Partners — Two Gene Keys that are holographically bonded together through opposition — in other words, they are exact mirror opposites. There are 32 such programming partners within the genetic matrix, and each creates a biofeedback loop that reinforces the themes of those Gene Keys at every level of frequency. At the Shadow frequency, the programming partners create physical, emotional and mental patterns and complexes that mutually reinforce each other. As awareness penetrates these patterns and transforms them, they release waves of creative energy at the Gift frequency, which in turn are mutually reinforced, leading to a continual raising of one's evolutionary frequency. At the Siddhic frequency, the programming partners no longer oppose each other but dawn as pure consciousness, creating a harmonic so pure that it deletes their difference.

Sequence — The means by which cellular transformation is unlocked and awakening is catalysed. As we learn to accept the Shadow frequencies in our lives, so we become witness to a progressive unlocking of the higher codes of consciousness within our bodies.

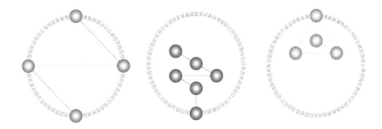

Shadow (Frequency) — The frequency band relating to all human suffering. The Shadow frequency band emerges from an ancient wiring in the human brain. Such wiring is based on individual survival and is linked directly to fear. The unconscious presence of fear in our system continues to enhance our belief that we are separate from the world around us. This deep-seated belief propagates a 'victim' mentality, since the moment we believe we are separate, we feel vulnerable and at the mercy of outside forces. When we live at the Shadow frequency band then we live within a culture of blame and shame. We blame those forces and people that we believe are outside us, and we feel shame when we believe we alone are responsible for our lives. Once you begin to understand how the Shadow frequency controls the majority of people in the world, including yourself, you realise how simple it is to move out of its grasp. Simply by shifting your attitude, you release the creative currents hidden within the Shadow frequencies and your life takes on a higher purpose. Your very suffering becomes the source of your salvation. Thus begins your journey away from those internal patterns and traits that keep you believing you are a victim and towards the inherent genius and love that is your true nature.

Siddhi (Frequency) — The frequency band relating to full embodiment and spiritual realisation. The very concept of frequencies and levels paradoxically dissolves when the Truth is realised as a Siddhi. The word 'siddhi' is from the Sanskrit meaning 'Divine Gift'. The siddhic state only comes about when all vestiges of the Shadow, particularly at a collective level, have been transformed into light. As you enter the state of Absorption, this alchemical transformation begins to accelerate, until finally, all falls silent and you enter the state of Embodiment at the Sixth Initiation. There are 64 Siddhis and each one refers to a different expression of Divine Realisation. Even though the realisation is the same in each case, its expression will differ and can even appear contradictory. The Siddhis spoken of in the Gene Keys Synthesis are not to be confused with the way they are understood in certain other mystical traditions. The 64 Siddhis are not obstacles on the path to realisation but are the very expression and fruition of realisation.

Sphere — In your Holgenetic Profile, a specific aspect of your life that has a corresponding Gene Key and line attributed to it. Providing focal points for ongoing contemplation the eleven spheres form the sequential steps along the Golden Path.

The Golden Path — The master genetic sequence for permanently raising your frequency from the Shadow to the Gift frequency. An integration of the Activation Sequence, the Venus Sequence and the Pearl Sequence, the Golden Path describes the natural unfolding of human awareness as it matures beyond the victim patterns of the Shadow frequency. All human beings sooner or later must walk some form of the Golden Path, as it symbolises the passage of the individuated 'soul' through the first four Initiations. As your lower three bodies (the physical, the astral and the mental) are gradually purified and brought into harmonic resonance, you will experience the opening of your heart and the releasing of your creative genius into the world. The Golden Path lays the foundation for living a high frequency life.

The Six Lines — Relating to the hexagram structure of the I Ching, the Six Lines describe further nuances of each of the 64 Gene Keys. If we see each Gene Key as a pre-designed archetypal picture, then each line is like the colour of that picture. Once you can see the colour, the whole picture comes alive. Knowing the six lines and their keynotes is an essential skill to master, as it enables you to interpret the many elements of the Hologenetic Profile in a simple and accessible way. There are many, many layers of keynotes for each of the six lines and they are fun to learn and illuminating to apply. The deeper you can feel the resonance of the six lines inside your being, the easier it is to understand your own sequences and share that resonance with others.

Transmutation — The process of dynamic and permanent change that comes about as you surrender and accept mutation. At the Shadow frequency, mutation is something that is greatly feared as it always challenges an established pattern, rhythm or routine. Unless mutations (periods of natural upheaval) are embraced and fully accepted in your life, transmutation cannot occur. Transmutation involves a complete shift from one state or plane to another.

After a transmutation, nothing is ever the same again. Transmutation only begins to occur at the Gift frequency band, as your deepest cellular victim patterns are transformed through awareness. Periods of intense mutation in your life are always a great opportunity for transmutation. So long as your attitude is open-hearted and accepting and you embrace and take responsibility for your own state, transmutation will occur in your life. With transmutation comes great clarity, freedom and creativity. It is the process through which your genius emerges into the world.

Venus Sequence — The primary genetic sequence for unlocking deep core emotional patterns in your life. As the central axis of the Golden Path, the Venus Sequence is an inner contemplative journey into the dynamics of your specific emotional wounding patterns, inherited through your ancestral DNA. Constructed from the positions of the earth, moon, Mars and Venus at the time of your birth, the Venus Sequence outlines a natural pathway of six Gene Keys which govern all your emotional patterns in this life. As your awareness begins to understand and observe the Shadow aspects of these six Gene Keys, particularly in your relationships, you will begin to transform the low frequency patterns into higher frequency Gifts. In this way, your astral body (your emotional nature) moves through a process of transmutation leading to the permanent opening of your heart.

During our current phase of evolution known as the Great Change, the Venus Sequence has particular relevance as its underlying purpose is to open up a new centre of awareness in the solar plexus.

3. THE PATHWAY OF CHALLENGE

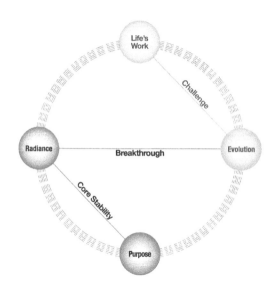

THE PATHWAY OF CHALLENGE

Our journey begins right away with a confrontation. In the Gene Keys, the central premise is that every Shadow contains a Gift, so we must begin by looking into the nature of the Shadows within us in order to get to the hidden Gift inside. This is your Challenge. It is the challenge that rings out inside every human being. Our lives are made or broken upon the back of this primal, archetypal challenge. When you come to the Gene Keys, you must be prepared for a certain level of inner discomfort, because to look into your Shadows and to become more aware of them in your daily life is what this work is all about.

In looking at your Challenge, you must look deeply into the dynamic between the 2 Gene Keys that straddle this Pathway. These are the two spheres of your Life's Work and your Evolution.

PROGRAMMING PARTNERS

An Allegory Of Consciousness

We are all here to evolve. It is written into the story of DNA that it must evolve in order to survive, and it must evolve even further in order to thrive. The two Gene Keys of your Life's Work and your Evolution are a genetic pairing, as are the two Gene Keys of your Radiance and Purpose. Of the three sequences of Gene Keys that make up this Golden Path, the Activation Sequence is unique in this respect. It consists of 2 pairs of opposites. In the language of the Gene Keys they are known as Programming Partners. When you look at the Gene Keys Hexagram Wheel below you will see that every Gene Key has another Gene Key exactly opposite from it. If you look at the structure of the 6 lines that make up those 2 hexagrams, you will see that they form the exact mirror pattern of each other. In the Gene Keys Synthesis we use this wheel as a means to locate moments of imprinting, for instance the time of one's birth.

EXAMPLE OF 2 PROGRAMMING PARTNERS IN THE HEXAGRAM WHEEL

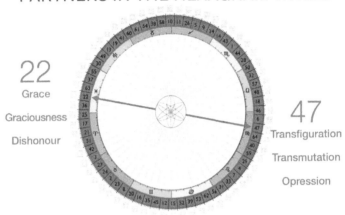

22
Grace

Graciousness

Dishonour

47
Transfiguration

Transmutation

Opression

Your Hologenetic Profile is calculated from the time and place of your birth and in particular from the position of the sun when you were born. And opposite the sun we find the earth, the place from which we look up into the heavens to locate our place in the space-time continuum. It is this polarity that we come into the world with, and they are known as your Life's Work and your Evolution. Your Life's Work is dictated symbolically by the sun, the yang force of energy, and your Evolution is dictated symbolically by the earth, the yin force of matter. Whereas your Life's Work is the expression of what you do, your Evolution is the turbine that drives what you do. The earthbound sphere of your Evolution tugging against that solar fire of your Life's Work is what sets up the basic tension that writes the script of your life.

All of the above can be understood as an allegory of how consciousness comes into the world. We are each an interplay of opposites – the seed from our father's line and the egg from our mother's line. When we convert this into the I Ching hexagram wheel, we have a beautiful timeless code to help us decipher the many myths that make up human destiny.

When you read the definition of the Programming Partners in the Glossary you can see that the 2 sets of Programming Partners that form your Activation Sequence represent mutually bonded codes buried deep within your DNA. The moment your awareness of the Shadow pattern unlocks these codes, an awakening event occurs as the stored tension of these oppositions is released inside you. This is why the very first pathway of the Golden Path is called the Pathway of Challenge – you have to dive right into the heart of that tension and release it at its core.

4. THE SPHERE OF YOUR LIFE'S WORK

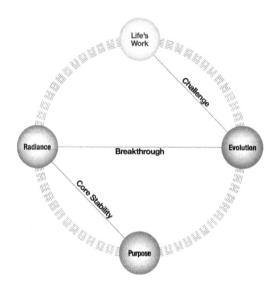

THE SPHERE OF YOUR LIFE'S WORK

You can begin by contemplating the Gene Key that represents your Life's Work. Your Life's Work is the tip of the iceberg of your entire profile. It is where your deeper purpose meets the outside world. There are many forms of work. Your outer work is one thing – what you are here to do in life – that is your career, job or daily role. This Gene Key is a good indicator of what you may be best suited to in the world. However, the Gene Keys are not literal. Rather they give you the frame of a storyline, and it is you who must fit this into an external role in your life. When you look at the Shadow of this Gene Key, you will see the pattern in your nature that prevents you from finding the kind of role that perfectly suits you.

The Shadow

The other kind of work is inner work. The Shadow of your Life's Work really shows you a challenge that you will meet over and over again in your life until you have fully accepted it. This is your inner Life's Work. There are essentially three phases that accompany the transformation of our Shadows. They are: Allow, Accept and Embrace. First you must begin to allow that this issue is in your life. You don't have to accept it right away. You may hate it, shy away from it or be enraged by it. But you must begin simply by allowing it to be there. And it may not be there all the time. You will have to watch for it.

Once you have allowed it you are ready to accept it, and acceptance is a beautiful thing. Acceptance means that your inner work is really kicking in. You have summoned the courage to take responsibility for something inside yourself. Acceptance sparks the fire of transformation and as the fire reddens around you, the final phase comes into play - the embrace. You take a deep breath and you let the Shadow in all the way. Only this totality allows a negative pattern to be fully transformed inside you. It is you fully opening your heart to the challenge of your life.

The Gift

Every Shadow contains a Gift. And this process of transformation takes time. We should be clear about this. You don't just transform this challenge and then move on to the next part of your Profile! This Challenge is there all the way along the journey. It is your primary challenge. As you continue to explore the inner reaches of your Hologenetic Profile, you will see how your embracing of this Pathway of Challenge opens up all the other doorways in your Profile, and there are other deeper Shadows lurking in there. But these in turn contain further Gifts. Every time you recognise a negative pattern and embrace it, you unlock another Gift. Ultimately each Gift is interrelated, just as each Shadow is interrelated. Your ongoing contemplation will reveal this to you. As the Gift comes out, so your Life's Work becomes clearer. Your inner work affects your outer work. This is a universal law.

The Siddhi

The Siddhi represents the Divine essence of your work in the world. As you contemplate the Shadow of your Life's Work, it is a good idea to counterbalance it by holding the Siddhi in mind and heart. You need to really consider this Siddhi and locate it as an essence inside yourself. It is what you are here to do. It is the essence of your biography. When your journey of contemplation brings you to the end of this Golden Path, you will return once more to this same Gene Key, but in another completely different octave. You need to hold this Siddhi in your heart throughout the journey, and by the end, if you are fortunate, it may have revealed itself to you in some form.

The specific words for the 64 Gene Keys are a set of linguistic keys. You may not at first understand them, but in time you may discover the stories, insights and vibrations that lie behind the words. One of your greatest allies in this journey will be patience.

Contemplating The 6 Lines

In the introduction to the Golden Path, we used the analogy of music to help understand the relationship between each Gene Key and its six lines. We said that if each Gene Key were a melody, then each line was like a key in which that melody could be played. In your Hologenetic Profile, you have a whole string of Gene Keys that relate to aspects of your consciousness, and each Gene Key comes with a specific line activation. A major part of your contemplation practise will be to unlock the inner meaning of your Gene Key and its line, in the context of its position within the overall sequence. Your Golden Path holds a potent storyline for the unfolding of your consciousness and the 6 lines provide an important part of your inner narrative. Their meanings are explored below.

THE 6 LINES OF THE LIFE'S WORK

Line 1 – The Creator

The 1st line of each Gene Key really expresses the inner essence of the archetype that it contains. We humans are here to be creative. Our Life's Work is essentially a creative work in process. When we finish our Life's Work and return to the void, someone else steps in to continue our work, whatever it may be, and so the chain of creative evolution continues. If you have a 1st line as your Life's Work then you are here to create something new. It has to be your idea – it has to be something that emerges from deep inside you. You can ride on the shoulders of other creators who have come before you, but still, your version must be an original. When you apply this line to your Life's Work Gene Key, you need to consider that Gene Key at a very deep level. Your contemplation must take you right to the bottom of the well. There is a great depth in you wanting to find expression in the world. You may need a lot of courage and patience to find and express yourself fully in your work. Whatever you do, it must have this vital creative element within it, otherwise you will never be able to feel fulfilled in your life.

Line 2 – The Dancer

Every 2nd line carries a strong feeling of fluidity in it. Whereas the 1st line is about digging down deep to unearth the creative fruits, the 2nd line is all about self-expression. At its best the 2nd line is also unselfconscious, like the dancer who becomes lost in the joy of the dance. If you have a 2nd line as your Life's Work, then you will have to find out the gifts in life that come to you naturally and easily. Early on in our lives it often becomes clear at school for example, which subjects we are best at, although we often end up being drawn down different paths. You need to do the things you are best at - the things you love – the things you can do without even thinking. The archetype of the dancer refers to an inherent natural gift that emanates from you. When you trust in this gift, it just flows out of you with a beautiful, natural unstudied air. When you contemplate the Gene Key of your Life's Work, think about the thing you do with the most grace and ease. This will give you a clue as to where your true Life's Work lies.

Line 3 – The Changer

Unlike the 2nd line that follows a clear inner flow out into the world, the 3rd line is far less predictable. All 3rd lines have change at their heart. They do not often manifest the kind of stability that the other lines have. This means that the lives of those with 3rd lines are often very colourful, or when viewed from the Shadow, chaotic. If you have a 3rd line for your Life's Work, your great challenge is to learn to let go of what your mind thinks is 'normal'. Your archetype is the Changer, which means that you will learn your Gifts from life. You may have many different experiences in different roles, with different people coming in and out of your life, and if you can let go and enjoy this kind of exciting narrative, then you will lead a very rich life. If however, you compare your life to others who may seem more stable, you may end up harbouring all manner of self-judgements that will undermine your true Gifts. When you contemplate the Gene Key of your Life's Work, you need to imagine it in its most dynamic, changing, adaptable form, and that will bring you closer to the essence of your Life's Work.

Line 4 – The Server

Of all the 6 lines, the 4th line has the capacity to be the most focussed. When you apply this line to the Gene Key of your Life's Work, it can create a very powerful, influential Gift. If you have the 4th line as your Life's Work, it colours the corresponding Gene Key with an incredible capacity for conviction. You have an innate ability to influence other people. Depending on your attitude, this can either push people away or draw them towards you. The realm of the 4th line is people, so it is important that you learn to listen to others. Whatever your Life's Work Gene Key, its healthiest expression is through service. For you, service can mean many things – it can for instance be about quality, refinement or courtesy, or it can be as obvious as being in a service profession. The Server is an archetype that clearly involves the giving of your Gifts for the sake of others. In other words, you are really in it because you love to see someone else smile.

Line 5 – The Fixer

There is a clear narrative flow through all the 6 lines. The 1st line discovers it, the 2nd line expresses it, the 3rd line experiments with it and adapts it, the 4th line spreads it, and then we come to the 5th line. The 5th line is pure practicality. It looks at the thing and decides whether it is going to really help the world or not. If it isn't then the 5th line just looks away, but if there is a chance that this thing may really be of use, then the 5th line will claim ownership of it and make something really powerful of it. If you have the 5th line for your Life's Work, then you have the capacity to go far in the outer world. The archetype of the fixer is about creating greater efficiency in the world. When you contemplate the Gene Key of your Life's Work, think about how you could make a business out of this archetype. Think about how you could use that as a leader. It doesn't mean you have to do that, but it allows your mind to function in the way nature intended. Your Gifts, when well organised, are needed by many people. Of all the 6 lines, you have perhaps the greatest capacity to be outwardly successful in the world through your Gifts.

Line 6 – The Teacher

The 6th line stands apart from the other lines. In a sense it lives according to different laws. This doesn't make it any better or worse, as each line has its advantages. The question that beats at the heart of all 6th lines is why? The 6th line has a certain relationship to the 1st line, as it brings completion to the whole spectrum of wisdom contained within each Gene Key. The 1st line holds the essence of the Gene Key and the 6th line writes its autobiography! In other words, the 6th line has the capacity to be the wisest of all the lines – not the smartest (1), not the most attractive (2), not the most exciting (3), not the most approachable (4), not the most successful (5) but the one that simply sees further than the others. This is the archetype of the Teacher, and as we have seen, this doesn't necessarily mean that if you have a 6th line for your Life's Work then you are destined to be a teacher. It means that you share the essential attribute of any really good teacher – you understand that people are all born with different gifts, and if you provide the right environment, then those gifts will always emerge on their own.

If you have the 6th line for the Gene Key of your Life's Work, then your contemplation of that Gene Key needs to be rooted in patience. In a way, you have to understand each of the approaches of the other 5 lines before you can answer the question why? The depth of this question means that your Gifts may take a long time to fully emerge in life. You have to be able to look back on your life and then you will begin to see through the eyes of wisdom. Contemplation is therefore a very natural path for you in life. It takes time, but in time, it always yields an answer.

5. THE SPHERE OF YOUR EVOLUTION

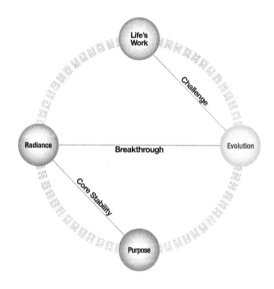

THE SPHERE OF YOUR EVOLUTION

Perhaps you have some inkling of the meaning of your Life's
Work from your initial contemplation. Perhaps it still seems a
mystery to you. Either is fine. This process of understanding
takes time. You can keep returning in your contemplation
to aspects of your Profile that do not quite make sense to
you. You can trust in the process of Self-Illumination. As you
continue to mull things over, sooner or later you will attain
clarity. We will now turn our lens to the next Sphere along
the Golden Path – the Sphere of Evolution. Your Evolution,
as we have seen, is in opposition to your Life's Work.
Together, these two spheres and their Gene Keys encapsulate
the primary challenge of your life. Look deeply then into the
Gene Key of your Evolution. It will very likely represent an
uncomfortable place for you.

The Shadow

It is essential that you fully understand the Shadow frequency
of the Gene Key relating to your Evolution. Until you come to
see it playing out in your life and begin the process of coming
to terms with it, your Activation Sequence will remain dormant.
There are several trigger points along the Golden Path and your
Evolution is the first. If you don't understand the meaning of
this Shadow or it doesn't seem to connect with you, then you
may need to consider it again from another angle. Sometimes
the words for the Gene Keys have more than one meaning. It is
also one thing to intellectually grasp a pattern, but quite another
to catch it in the present moment.

Often these patterns emerge in the mirror of our relationships,
and often they have become a part of our behaviour or they
motivate our behaviour. One thing is certain, the moment
you experience uncertainty or pain, this Shadow will be close
by. You can make that your first project – wait until you next
experience a challenge – it can be inner or outer – and then be
vigilant for this Shadow. Once you have encountered it, you
will most likely know it very well.

The Gift

Treading the Golden Path may not be the easiest thing you attempt in life, but it is well worth the effort. Your first challenge is to understand your challenge! When you contemplate these two Programming Partners – your Life's Work and your Evolution together, you may begin to see how entrenched is that challenge. However your Evolution is not about getting past this challenge because it is the discomfort that shows us that we are growing. The secret is to learn to appreciate your specific challenge in life. Your Gifts, that is your genius, grow out of the compost of these Shadow patterns and it is your awareness that transforms them. Take a good look at the Gift of your Evolution and you may see a quality that sets you apart from others. There are only 64 Gene Keys so there will be many people with this same Gene Key for their Evolution, but when you add in each of the nuances along the rest of your Golden Path you will have begun to decipher the story of your destiny. The Gift is what emerges as you change your whole attitude to life by not allowing yourself to behave as though you were a victim. In addition to this, your Evolutionary Gift grounds you in your physical body. It is a great leveller as it makes you feel an equal with every other human being. We all come into the world with a challenge, and our willingness to embrace that challenge determines the strength of our spirit.

The Siddhi

It is important to consider these Programming Partners – the 2 Gene Keys of your Life's Work and your Evolution - as a single field of consciousness that dictates your genius. You can consider the Shadows, the Gifts and the Siddhis of all the Programming Partners like that. When you come to the Siddhi, this quality denotes the potential expression of your life as a fully realised, enlightened human being. In the Gene

Keys, we hold an inner image of the Siddhis as a counter to our Shadows. The Siddhis are not a promise, and we also need to be careful of being caught up in the trap of hope. If you hope for these qualities, you are subtly playing into the game of being a victim. The Siddhi of your Evolution is an essence inside you.

It fuels the essence of what you are here to do in life. It is a special dispensation you were gifted with at birth, and at times in your life it will come to the fore. The deeper you accept the Shadow patterns, the humbler you will feel on the inside because the Siddhis arise out of intense feelings of gratitude. They well up at key points in our life, and the challenges we face can bring forth those precious moments when we glimpse the truth of what we are.

CONTEMPLATING YOUR EVOLUTION

When the revelation of the Hologenetic Profile first came into being it was offered as a personal consultation or 'reading'. Because another person explained your Profile to you it always came second-hand, in someone else's words. While this served its purpose at the time, it didn't allow for the real beauty of this knowledge to emerge as it was intended. It took some time to realise that the Gene Keys and the Golden Path are tools for Self Illumination. They come alive inside you as you contemplate them. Rather than receive the wisdom second-hand, you now have all the tools you need to unlock it for yourself, inside yourself. A single insight that arises naturally from inside your own psyche is of greater benefit to you than all the wisdom given to you by another person, whoever they may be.

As you begin to contemplate the Gene Keys that comprise your Golden Path, you will do well to bear the above point in mind. This is your voyage and it will take as long as you need it to take. If you are patient, you will give your intuition the space it needs to absorb the knowledge, digest it and draw out the energetic nutrients your soul needs. As you apply your specific Line activations to your Gene Keys, it's worth reading and considering all the 6 Lines, even the ones that don't seem to apply directly to you. The lines all tell the same story, and knowing this story helps you to locate your particular place within the whole.

THE 6 LINES OF YOUR EVOLUTION

Line 1 – Self And Empowerment

In the sphere of one's Life's Work, the 1st line is keynoted 'the Creator'. In the sphere of one's Evolution, this becomes all about the empowerment of the Self. Your Activation Sequence is about discovering your genius in life, regardless of which line you have activated. If you have a 1st line Evolution then your primary challenge is always likely to be about how self-assured or inadequate you feel. As a creative type you may sometimes feel you are your own worst enemy. Yours is a private path. That doesn't mean you cannot seek outside help and support, but it does suggest that the answers need to come from inside you. The arc of your evolution depends upon you digging deeply into your own aloneness and finding sustenance in there. No one else can empower you or dis-empower you. You can only do these things for yourself. When you meet this challenge courageously, then your Gifts will always empower others to find the same inner strength inside them. This is something to contemplate alongside the Gene Key of your Evolution.

Line 2 – Passion And Relationships

Whereas the 1st line contains the secret essence of the Gene Key, the 2nd line is all about expressing this essence. If the 1st line were a seed, then the 2nd line would represent the sapling. The 2nd line therefore has a very different set of challenges.

This is about the uninhibited expression of energy as passion, and passion always catches the eye of others. When you contemplate the Gene Key of your Evolution, imagine how you might express these qualities with passion. Imagine the Shadow expressed through anger, without realisation of the consequences. This may well tell the story of some of your relationship difficulties in life. The 2nd line always learns most intensely through a relationship. The dilemma and the beauty of the 2nd line as a life theme is that its nature is to be unselfconscious. At the Gift and Siddhi frequency this emerges gracefully and has enormous beneficial impact, but at the Shadow frequency it is disastrous. Negative energy expressed unselfconsciously, whether through actions or words, is always destructive.

If you therefore have a 2nd line theme as your Life's Work and Evolution, your challenge is to listen to and observe the feedback from those closest to you. They always provide a very clear mirror of the frequency moving through you. Eventually, you will become so attuned to your environment that you will stop yourself before a negative pattern is even expressed. Then your true passion will emerge innocently and be met with acceptance and gratitude.

Line 3 – Energy And Experience

You may recall that the 3rd line is all about change. When you are contemplating a 3rd line Evolution, you need to look at this Gene Key as a journey. How will you spend this genetic inheritance you have been gifted? For you life is all about the experience rather than the result. Whether an endeavour appears to succeed or fail, it's all about the journey and the experience that you have learned through it. Let's look at the 56th Gene Key with its Shadow of Distraction and Gift of Enrichment as an example.

If we were contemplating a 1st line theme here it would be all about being distracted by inner issues inside oneself, for example fears and/or obsessions. If it were a 2nd line, the distraction would be relationships, and if it were a 3rd line, it would be experiences. So you might be the kind of person who is drawn to one experience after another as a distraction from that which really enriches your spirit. When you finally let go of the idea that you are going to get something from all those experiences, then you begin to realise that you have actually learned a great deal along the way. Then you can use your experiences (good and bad) to enrich others, and this becomes your Gift. When you apply the lines to the Gene Keys in this way, the story of your life often comes into new perspective.

Line 4 – Love And Community

With a 4th Line Evolution, your life's great challenge is likely to be about finding a balance between being alone and being with others. How will you combine your need to be of service with your need to have space? At the Shadow frequencies the 4th line has a tendency to simply go to one extreme or the other and then either collapse from exhaustion or end up being cut off from others.

With the 4th line the theme is always love – the love of being with friends and the love of one's own company. In a rich life, love flows freely between these two poles in a natural and easy rhythm. As a 4th line, you might like to view the Gene Key of your Evolution as a quality designed to be shared with others. The more you share your Gift, the more you feed yourself and the more influential you become. The gift of the 4th line is to touch people's hearts and bring them over to one's point of view, so long as it is the most ethical point of view. Of all the 6 lines, you are the one most equipped to convince others of the importance of a heart-based approach to any situation.

In addition to this, your 4th line perspective is adept at communication, which makes you a powerful force in any community or business.

Line 5 – Power And Projection

The 5th line Evolution is all about the projection and use of power. As a 5th line you have a built-in 'X factor' – a kind of mystique that emerges through your aura. This is not something that you can do anything about because it is uncultivated. Therefore you have to be very aware of the profound effect you have on others. People will naturally be drawn to you, no matter what you stand for. At the Shadow frequencies this almost always ends in disappointment, both for you and others. Unless you are aware of your power you are likely to be misinterpreted by others, so one of the most important things for you is to learn how and when to express yourself. When you are passionate about something you can be captivating to others and they may harbour all kinds of hidden projections about you that have no foundation in reality. What this means is that the 5th line has to learn about personal and professional boundaries. When you express yourself with economy and clarity you minimise the risk of misunderstanding. When considering the Gene Key of your Evolution think about how easily others could misunderstand this great gift. Then you will be able to take full advantage of your 5th line projection field.

Line 6 – Education And Surrender

The 6th line lives out a very rich narrative over the course of its life. Unlike any of the other lines it moves through the whole story of the lines in a single lifetime! For the 6th line there is so much to learn before one's dreams can come true. In addition, by the time you have matured enough in wisdom, your understanding of your own dreams will have changed. This is why surrender is one of the keynotes of the 6th line Evolution.

You will need to learn to trust in the fates. When you apply the 6th line theme to the Gene Key of your Evolution, it may help to look at it as a maturing quality.

The 6th line is all about the long-term view. This is why education is such an important part of your life. Through your own experience you will learn that life knows best in the end, and it is this trust in life that you can eventually bring into the world as a role model. Education does not impose views – rather it draws out that which is already inside. This 6th line adds a quality to any Gene Key that lends it a great kudos in the world. This is something deeper than success or influence in the world. It has more to do with investment in a greater future for us all. In this sense the 6th line is willing to sacrifice personal goals for a wider, collective goal, and even one that will not mature until long after one's own lifetime.

6. THE PATHWAY OF BREAKTHROUGH

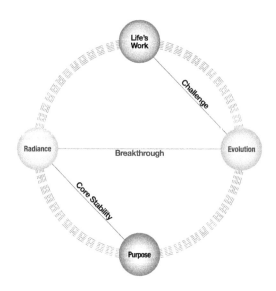

THE PATHWAY OF BREAKTHROUGH

Flowing out of the first Pathway of Challenge emerges the next step along the Golden Path – the Pathway of Breakthrough. As we have seen, every Shadow contains a Gift, and this is epitomised here in the dynamic archetype of breakthrough. Once you begin to allow, accept and embrace your inner Shadows, then a miracle occurs – something that was hidden inside you breaks out. The breakthrough is always there waiting inside us. Our Evolution depends upon breakthroughs. Genes themselves evolve through unexpected breakthroughs called mutations, and many mutations over time lead to a transmutation - the emergence of a completely new form or behaviour.

It is your ongoing contemplation and the increased awareness that comes with it that triggers a breakthrough. Awareness is a powerful catalyst for change – indeed it is a prerequisite of transformation. The purpose of the Golden Path is to reflect to you the major issues that underpin your daily patterns, physical, emotional and mental. In this mirror you will see more deeply into the forces that drive your outer destiny.

When you look at your Hologenetic Profile you will notice that the Pathway of Breakthrough bridges the 2 pairs of programming partners that comprise your Activation Sequence. The Life's Work and the Evolution represent the outermost edge of your life as it flows into form. In contrast, the Radiance and the Purpose represent the unconscious forces that motivate and drive the patterns of your outer Prime Gifts. This is why this second Pathway engenders a breakthrough.

As your awareness burrows deeper into the Shadow patterns, it unlocks something that was previously hidden from you. When we refer to the light in your DNA, or the 'higher purpose hidden in your DNA', this is what we are referring to.

There is a great deal of potential energy stored up within those genetic coils inside us.

The Activation Sequence is about discovering our genius in life. This genius, as we will see, is less about a role or skill and more about a quality of consciousness.

It emerges as a rush that passes through the physical body. How it is experienced is up to the individual. For some it comes all in one go, whereas for others it emerges over time. For most people, the breakthrough is an ongoing process. It is a 'breaking through' that comes and goes as your contemplation deepens. Some breakthroughs are experienced as mental insights – for example a breakthrough when a pattern of denial suddenly comes to an end. Other breakthroughs seem purely emotional, and can lead to intense emotional states and feelings, often accompanied by tears. However you experience your breakthrough, you should know that it is primarily physical. It begins as an explosion of light somewhere in the cellular world within.

7. THE SPHERE OF YOUR RADIANCE

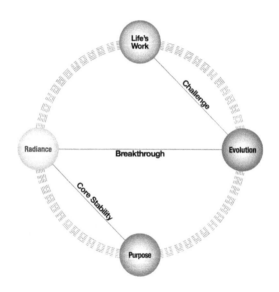

THE SPHERE OF YOUR RADIANCE

You may wonder why and how we can have light locked away inside us. It may seem fantastical or even whimsical. The truth is that every form in the universe is made of light. The emptiness around the form is the darkness from which the form arises as light. The two principles belong to one another, constantly giving birth to each other and at the same time defining each other. In your form, the body which lies wrapped around you as you read these words, a great inner light is burning. Physical evolution occurs as this light moves collectively through all human forms, driving us forward in understanding, urging us not only to survive but also to thrive as a species. However, spiritual evolution underpins physical evolution. In fact both forms of evolution are part of a single principle, with spiritual evolution as the seed and physical evolution following as the fruit.

Spiritual evolution emerges in individuals as breakthrough. The inner light finds its way out of our DNA and floods our physical bodies. This is what we refer to as your Radiance. Your Radiance dictates your health, your vitality and something even more nebulous – your aura. Your aura is the electromagnetic afterglow of your inner essence. It cannot be seen directly with the naked eye, but can be sensed by human intuition. Your Radiance also acts as the hidden instrument of your intuition. It warns you of potential threats in the energetic environment around you. Like a GPS 'satnav' it guides you in finding the right experiences and people in life.

The Shadow

The Shadow of your Radiance is one of the most powerful internal forces that can undermine your life. When you contemplate your Radiance, you must look deeply into this pattern because it probably represents an inner motivating force that lies outside your conscious grasp. When this

Shadow is allowed to govern your life then you will find yourself out of kilter with the basic rhythms of life. The earth and all life forms move according to a deep heartbeat known as the Schumann Resonance. This is a measurable pulse that underpins all organic life.

Most modern human beings live lives that are out of synchronisation with this organic pulse, which puts our bodies under stress and weakens our immune system. It also exerts a subtle influence over the way we behave in our daily lives, resulting in a worried, hurried lifestyle and a time-centric outlook rooted in an unconscious mistrust in the natural flow of life.

The Gift

One of the first signs that your Radiance is breaking through is that you naturally begin to slow down inside yourself and in your daily life. You become a more contemplative individual. This doesn't necessarily mean that you think more about things – rather it involves you becoming much more settled inside your skin. You begin to move in harmony with the earth, so you immediately become more grounded. Your Radiance emerges as a pulsing of light through your aura, and the more you learn to align your body with the Schumann Resonance then the more your Gifts come to the fore. The emergence of your Radiance has two main effects on your life. Firstly, you will become more healthy because you feel more healthy on the inside. Your Radiance will tend to guide you towards healthier habits, which can be a part of your breakthrough. And of course, being healthy you will feel happier – but not for any external reason – your endocrine system sends signals throughout your body that all is well, which results in the release of endorphins for example.

The second effect of your Radiance is to catalyse good fortune through the principle of synchronicity. Being in harmony with the wider quantum environment unlocks the higher purpose within your DNA, and your true destiny begins to unravel.

The Siddhi

The Siddhi of your Radiance is an emanation that breaks through from the essence of your being. There are states of consciousness beyond what we refer to as genius. Genius is a manifestation of the activation of your Gifts. Beyond your Gifts lies the realm of the Siddhis, which we might refer to as 'Divine Gifts'. The Siddhi of your Radiance is not an easy thing to put into words.

Throughout human history we have heard stories of human beings who have shone with an inner light or radiance. In iconic religious art we often see images of saints or buddhas with aureoles around their heads. Such images are not only emblematic, but many are based upon real life accounts of phenomena that occurred to living human beings. In the modern age since the Industrial Revolution where so many people live lives out of harmony with the greater rhythms of existence, we only rarely see examples of the phenomenon of true Radiance. As you contemplate your Radiance, hold inside yourself the possibility of such states. This alone will help raise the frequency of your aura.

THE 6 LINES OF YOUR RADIANCE

Line 1 – Solitude

The 1st line Radiance requires solitude in order to achieve breakthrough. However, solitude must not come as an enforcement. It must become a deep love. When you look into the Gene Key of your Radiance, if it is a 1st line, consider how the Shadow may unsettle your inner quiet.

Solitude is not an extreme – rather it is an inner state. You can be in a healthy relationship and still enjoy endless solitude. When the poet Rilke said: 'to walk around inside yourself and meet no one for hours' this is what he was talking about. The more deeply you relax into your Radiance, the more alone you become and at the same time the more connected you become. It is a wonderful paradox. All Radiance, no matter which line it is filtered through, begins its breakthrough by means of a deep love of solitude. The measure of your Radiance is how close it makes you feel to others rather than how distant. This is a statement worthy of deep contemplation. If you have a 1st line Radiance then you will doubtless need to spend time in physical solitude, and this may also have an effect on where and how you choose to live.

Line 2 – Marriage

Although the 2nd line Radiance is keynoted 'Marriage', this may not be a literal interpretation. All 2nd lines thrive in one-to-one relationships, but that can mean many things.

Your Radiance requires biofeedback rather than simply emerging in solitude like the 1st line. This means that your Radiance may emerge when you are in nature, or when you are in movement or both. You simply need to be in an intense relationship with something or someone. When you look at the Gene Key of your Radiance, contemplate how it might naturally flow into some kind of relationship in your life. What do you love doing? Who do you love being with? What will you marry your life force with? These are the questions to contemplate because these are the possible outlets for your Radiance. 2nd lines often find one thing or one person or one place that lights them up, and until you give your attention to that relationship, your Radiance will remain in a sense unplugged.

Line 3 – Interaction

Like the 2nd line, the 3rd line Radiance also needs biofeedback but in a totally different way. The 3rd line needs diversity and change as opposed to the 2nd line needing exclusivity. If you have a 3rd Line Radiance, you will probably thrive when on the move. You may love to travel, or you may love a place because it offers so much diversity. The 3rd line is also likely to enjoy the urban environment with its many possibilities as much as the wilderness. For you, Radiance is all about interaction. It's not so much about the results of the interaction but the exchange itself – whether that is ideas, experiences, knowledge, business etc. The 3rd line Radiance needs to be in the thrill of life. It needs to move through all manner of experiences and yet without becoming overly attached to any single experience. Your breakthrough may come as you let go of the idea of having goals or expectations and simply enjoy swimming through the many phases of your life. Having a 3rd line Radiance will take you through all kinds of life experiences, which taken together may make you a very compassionate person. For this reason, many people with 3rd lines find themselves helping those less fortunate than themselves.

Line 4 – Friendship

The 4th line Radiance represents the path of the humanitarian. This is a Radiance rooted in aloneness, but that is directed outwards towards helping others, and specifically people. With a 4th line Radiance you will have a magnetic ability to draw people towards yourself. Ironically at the Shadow frequency this works against you because you will draw those people towards you who are not healthy for you. However, at the higher frequencies you can be the focal point for all manner of talented people. If you have a 4th line Radiance this makes you potentially a very influential person in the world, and the purer your aspirations, the further your reach will travel. On a personal level, your body thrives when you are in the company of those you love and trust. The worst thing you can therefore do is cut yourself off from your community. Because of its approachability the 4th line often has the most refined people skills and thrives working in teams. At its highest level, the Radiance of the 4th line can reach out and open up the hearts of other people.

Line 5 – Impact

The 5th line Radiance has a higher purpose designed to have a wide impact in society. Of all the lines, the 5th line Radiance is the most beguiling and mysterious. If you have a 5th line Radiance other people will always sense that there is something special about you, and that you may be able to help them in some way. It doesn't matter what your outer role is – people are really drawn to the inner essence. If you shy away from your power, you will therefore be hiding your light under a bushel. As a 5th line, you may feel that others have an unrealistic expectation of you, and this may be true, but you shouldn't let it stop you from having a positive impact in the world. You are a born leader, and your Gift will always seek a practical outlet. As long as you are crystal clear with yourself and others about what you are promising, then your reputation will continue to grow.

The 5th line has a great potential in our current technological age, since it naturally has a global reach. As you contemplate your Gifts you could consider how you might use them in this way to bring beneficial change and transformation to your chosen sphere.

Line 6 – Nurture

If you have a 6th line Radiance then you probably hold a dream deep inside you. This dream may be something that has grown with you since you were young, and it is a dream that requires continual nurturing. Your dream will go through many mutations over the course of your life, and it is important not to give up hope. Your Radiance contains the necessary energetic ingredients of magnetism and experience to bring about the fulfilment of your dream. With a 6th line you may not even have a clear picture of the dream inside you, although you probably sense its presence. You therefore have to be very patient as the dream unfolds. Every experience that comes your way is an opportunity to polish the dream and give it more definition. Some experiences may even appear to shatter the form of the dream in order that it can be reformed in a clearer and more practical way. As a 6th line Radiance your Gift is designed to emerge over the long term – as an impulse at the cutting edge of human evolution. Because of this, you must take the long-term view and continue to nurture your deep intent of being of service to the whole. In time, the dream will then manifest and your role within the bigger picture will become completely clear, both to yourself and to others.

8. THE PATHWAY OF CORE STABILITY

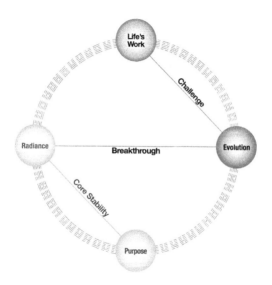

THE PATHWAY OF CORE STABILITY

Core Stability is the potential reward of breakthrough. The Activation Sequence is based on how you deal with the challenges of your life. No matter who you are or where you live, life will always throw challenges at you. This fact is written into evolution itself. We must embrace change or we will falter. The way we handle the challenge of change determines whether it becomes breakthrough, breakdown or break-up. The Gene Keys teach us that our potential to thrive in life depends on maintaining a high frequency attitude and this comes about as we own, understand and accept our Shadow tendencies. When we are able to do this, our challenges make us stronger and more grounded rather than resentful and more downtrodden. Every time we allow a Shadow pattern to be transformed a little more of our genius incarnates into the world.

The Pathway of Core Stability is about becoming more rooted and comfortable in your physical body. It is about becoming more aligned with the deep magnetic currents that move through and around the earth. Rather than making you more solid, it makes you more able to adjust your position appropriately in relation to outer and inner events. Core Stability denotes inner strength. Internally it is about responding to life rather than reacting to life. Externally Core Stability has less to do with muscular power and more to do with the tensile, flexible strength of sinew, tendon and even bone. Socially, Core Stability requires a deep honouring of one's ancestry and culture while at the same time seeing beyond the confines of these things. Core Stability is a state of dynamic equilibrium and compassionate clarity that results whenever a person begins to live and move from their deep core.

The Pathway of Core Stability connects the 2 programming partners known as your Radiance and your Purpose. These 2 spheres and their Gene Keys represent the unconscious forces that propel you along the line of your destiny.

Like a surfer riding a giant wave, you must learn to consistently adjust your posture, balance and direction to meet the unpredictable primal surge of nature beneath you. Before Breakthrough can occur a deep impulse of awareness must reach through into the ocean depths of your unconscious. This is what happens when you squarely face your challenges in life without behaving as though you are a victim. You break through into the deepest recesses of your unseen potential and you unlock the light that lies there. Core Stability is both a process and a birthright. You must claim the birthright of your true Purpose rather than squander it through compromise and fear. Each of us is here to do something powerful, and the Pathway of Core Stability is the inner conduit along which that power and purpose will one day emerge.

9. THE SPHERE OF YOUR PURPOSE

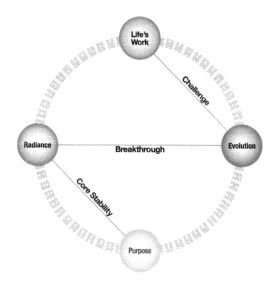

THE SPHERE OF YOUR PURPOSE

When we reach deep down inside ourselves, we always arrive at the question of purpose. One of the extraordinary traits of humans is to ask this question: what is my purpose? Perhaps we only ask this question when we are not yet fulfilling our highest purpose. The Gene Keys speak of higher purpose as opposed to just purpose. When we contemplate the question of our purpose we often think of it in terms of what we are here to do. Doing however is only the by-product of our being. Here at the foot of the Pathway of Core Stability and at the root of the Activation Sequence itself lies a potential answer to our oldest question.

Purpose is not about what we are here to do. It is about the quality of our consciousness. When you begin to contemplate the Gene Key that relates to your Purpose, think about it as the aroma of your deepest inner essence. Your true Purpose lies beyond your conscious reach as it lies hidden in your DNA. Your Purpose is designed to be unlocked by life. It calls upon you to evolve through your challenges and it emerges progressively over the course of your life as you move through breakthrough and transformation.

Your Purpose has another unique quality – it represents the essence of your humanity, of your beautiful ordinariness and your love of being alive inside a physical body on the physical plane. When you look at the 6 lines of the Purpose you will notice that they all concern aspects and elements of the workings of your physical body. As a human being, your Purpose is to fill your body with your consciousness – your deepest purpose is simply to be.

The Shadow

One of the hardest things for a human being to experience is the simple wonder of being. How often in a day do you simply stop what you are doing and witness a moment of pure being? The Shadow of your Purpose prevents you from experiencing such moments, and as you awaken more to your Purpose you may be surprised how often such moments arise and how easy it is to miss them.

When you contemplate the Gene Key that relates to your Purpose, consider how its Shadow works at an unconscious level to pull you away from the simple joy of being alive. Because of the depth of this Shadow pattern it is often hard for you to see it at work, but it will tend to consistently unsettle you. At the Shadow level of frequency you will not feel at home in your body, and you will certainly not feel stable and calm.

Core Stability is about being able to respond, but at the Shadow frequency we do not respond – we react – we react out of our instability because we do not feel safe and aligned with our core or with nature. Reaction also perpetuates the low frequency pattern in the world because it tends to trigger other people's instability. Thus it is a rare thing to meet a person living out their higher purpose in life. Many people may think they are doing so, but the real thing is unmistakeable. You will see a person living a life from a place of deep-seated calm. You will see a person utterly at home in the world, with a compassionate understanding of the suffering of others, and somewhere deep within them you may sense an inner smile of empathic humour and profound fulfilment. As you contemplate your own Purpose, these are good qualities to bear in mind!

The Gift

If you really want to get in tune with your deepest Purpose in life, there is one failsafe way to do it – spend more time listening to nature. Our Core Stability is about feeling the pulse of the earth within us. At the core of the earth is a liquid metal fire generating an electromagnetic field that influences all life forms on our planet. As your Life's Work is a symbolic reflection of the outer sun, so your Purpose is a symbolic reflection of this secret inner fire at the heart of the earth. Your Gifts emerge as you attune to that which is hidden inside you. To access this unconscious realm, you must heed the archetypes and myths that stir your spirit and the examples of other lives that have inspired you. Your Purpose connects you strongly with the past, with your ancestral DNA and the culture you were born into. Our Gifts are grounded in the memory of our personal and collective past.

It is a sobering fact that our Gifts only emerge as we come to terms with our past, as we learn to forgive and accept those Shadow patterns that we may have inherited from our parents and grandparents. As you will learn, your Purpose represents another portal that leads into the Venus Sequence, the master code for unlocking all the emotional patterns rooted in our past. But before we set off on that next phase of the voyage along the Golden Path, we need to first of all achieve a certain level of inner calm. We need to witness the Gift of our Purpose coming alive within our physical body rather than simply sensing it as a mental concept. Until we can physically touch this Gift and feel it bringing us a new level of Core Stability, we are not ready for that next step into the volatile realm of the emotional plane.

The Siddhi

The Siddhi of your Purpose is special. It is like a gift given to you by the gods so that you may bring it to the earth. The purpose of this gift is always healing. This Siddhi is the reason for your incarnation as it underpins everything that you are here to do in life. As such it is the very heart of your genius. In the great legends of old, we may recall stories of treasure or crystals hidden in underground vaults deep in the earth.

Often this treasure is guarded by some mythical creature such as a dragon, which must then be fought and vanquished. The Siddhi of your Purpose is an emanation of the earth itself. It is an ideal you are here to bring onto the physical plane. You must therefore go inwards and downwards through the Shadow to find this inner essence, and your whole life is an odyssey to mine this gold.

Those of us who are privileged enough to have time to contemplate our purpose have a special responsibility to the earth to bring this essence into the world. There still exists much suffering in the world, and every time we incarnate even a small aspect of the greater ideal of a better world, we fulfil our higher Purpose. At the level of frequency of the Siddhis your Purpose is no longer your Purpose. It becomes a selfless collective impulse to serve the whole.

When you contemplate the Siddhi of your Purpose you are touching the deepest most hidden possibility of your life. If you were to contemplate nothing else, this alone would be enough to bring a powerful transformation into your life.

THE 6 LINES OF YOUR PURPOSE

Line 1 – Physicality (bones)

You may recall that the 1st line of your Radiance is about needing solitude in order to attain breakthrough. This solitude further requires that you pay special attention to your physical body in life. The body has often been likened to a temple, and this is exactly how the 1st line needs to view it. If you have a 1st line Purpose then the quality of this Gene Key has to be anchored deeply into your physicality. Yours will also be a very physical life, where the health and vitality of the body is paramount. At the same time this is not only about being pure, but about balancing health with sensual enjoyment. With a 1st line Purpose you are here to enjoy being alive – to enjoy good food and physical activity, to get your feet wet by involving yourself in things of the earth, like a blissful dog rolling in the wet grass. You will see that this line is also about the bones, the structural element of human physicality. The bones are crystalline, connecting us to our ancestry like a powerful tuning fork that ripples with memory. With a 1st line Purpose you are called upon to be a record keeper for the mysteries of the past. That which emerges in the future requires your foundation in order for it to survive and thrive.

Line 2 – Posture (fluids)

Each of the 6 lines builds upon the foundation of the line that comes before it. Thus the 2nd line brings movement and flow into the structure of the body and bones. The secret of the 2nd line Purpose is the spine. It is through the spine that you find your Core Stability, and your spine dictates your physical posture. Genius for example does not flow out into the world through a stooped posture. Genius sings out through the body, coming from our inner alignment with the earth's core. The strength of the spine is in its flexibility, and your Radiance emerges out of the fluidity of your Purpose. This does not mean that your Purpose is always changing – rather that it is fulfilled through the joy you derive from being in a body that is constantly responding to your environment. The 2nd line is an expression of structure as flow, as opposed to stillness. At the same time flow often also involves stillness in the shape of pauses. When you contemplate the Gene Key of your Purpose through the 2nd line, this Gift can only emerge as you learn to let your body follow its deep inner fluidic rhythms. To be in harmony with life is to always find the path of effortlessness, and this is the essence of the 2nd line's great gift.

Line 3 – Movement (blood)

Change is the essence of the teaching contained in the I Ching, and the 3rd line is the great rider of the currents of change. When the 3rd line manifests through your Purpose then your Core Stability comes through movement and energy rather than stillness. This is not the effortless flow of the 2nd line but a dynamic and electrical energy burst that propels you into a life of action. The 3rd line is symbolised by the flow of blood within your body, which depends upon movement and change. Yours is a life rich in travel, adventure and experience. The 3rd line Purpose also needs regular physical exertion and exercise in order to feel alive and grounded. It is through physical exercise that you find your connection to the earth and its rhythms. Blood flows everywhere within the body, and your Purpose comes alive as you move through the many changing scenes of your destiny, from encounter to encounter. For many people the idea of stability is connected to consistency, but for a 3rd line Purpose, consistency can be a force that traps you. This is not to be confused with commitment. Commitment is vital for each of the 6 lines, but within commitment you can also build in change and adaptation.

Line 4 – Breath (rhythm)

It is interesting to contemplate each of the 6 lines of the Purpose regardless of which appears in your Hologenetic Profile. Each line is an aspect of Core Stability so they apply to us all. The lines simply show which of the 6 themes is highlighted more in our lives. Here the 4th line becomes about the breath and its ability to bring us into harmony with a deeper life rhythm.

The air that moves into your body is the same air that moves into all other living bodies, so at a primal level, our breath is what connects us to each other. The 4th line has a gift for connecting with others – with people or creatures. If you have a 4th line Purpose, then this will tend to move you naturally into communion with others. Your very Core Stability comes from connecting through friendship and service. The times you may feel most at home in your body and on the earth are likely to be when you are surrounded by those whom you love. The 4th line Purpose is felt as a profound urge to bring others into harmony, to bring others together in the same breath pattern. When you bring people together, after some time the group will develop its own unique breath pattern, and this can be an extraordinary experience. It is the great potential of the 4th line to bring humanity together into the realisation of our unity.

Line 5 – Voice (frequency)

With the 5th line, we move from the respiratory to the nervous system, and from the breath to the voice. The 5th line uses the rhythm of the breath and adds vibration and tone to it. This is all about the human voice. When you consider the 5th line Purpose you are seeing a Gift that must be spoken and shared. The 4th line is about the heart-to-heart connection, which can be communicated verbally or non-verbally. The 5th line is about having an impact, and this means that the essence of the Purpose must be vibrated as a frequency. If you have a 5th line Purpose then your Core Stability is connected to the way you communicate with others. If you are having a bad day you will find that everything you say simply makes things worse, because it is through your frequency that you either gain or lose your Core Stability. It is always possible for you to regain Core Stability through using tone, for example through chanting or singing. This can instantly bring you back into alignment with your Purpose as a living energetic field. The other aspect of your Purpose is to use your voice in some way to bring organisation or improvement to a particular sphere of life. This is Purpose fulfilled through some form of leadership.

Line 6 – Intent (cells)

When we reach the 6th line, Purpose can be understood as a cellular awareness that is streamed throughout the physical body. The 6th line always brings the story of the lines to a conclusion. It is in our cells that our frequency is anchored, whether that is a Shadow frequency or the highest Siddhic emanation. If you have a 6th line Purpose then your fulfilment comes through the realisation that your aura is the thing that really does the talking. Although the 5th line brings Purpose into the world through language and tone, the 6th line offers it through a sense of presence. Regardless of how you express Purpose, you convey it through the intent of the frequency of your aura. Each of the 6 lines of the Purpose has to do with a different manifestation of awareness in the physical body. The 6th line brings the awareness deep into the cells of every corner of the physical body where it is experienced as an energetic field that surrounds the body. This is the aura. As a sense of Purpose this extends the awareness away from the sense of separateness that comes from pure physicality into the potential future of a new kind of human awareness. This new awareness is the evolutionary intent to experience the unity of all life.

THE ACTIVATION SEQUENCE AND THE PURPOSE OF LIFE

As you journey deeper into your Activation Sequence you may begin to realise something rather special about the real purpose of your life, and indeed the purpose of all life. When you experience an authentic breakthrough through your contemplation, rather than making you feel somehow 'higher', it brings you further down to earth. You will find yourself settling more into the soft shell of your physical body. The purpose of the Activation Sequence is to release this deeper breath from within your belly and to help you remember that the purpose we are really seeking is to be found in our body in a simple state of relaxed awareness and presence.

The Gene Keys speak of higher purpose as the realisation of a quality of consciousness unique to our body and our chemistry. The consciousness is the same but the experience and the lens for the consciousness are different from person to person. There is a beautiful subtle quality about you that sets you apart from all others, and when you breathe the memory of this back into your being then you begin to have a sense of what the word Purpose really means.

There is a pathway in your Hologenetic Profile that goes directly from your Purpose to your Life's Work, and although this is not one of the strands that make up the journey of the Golden Path, it is an integrative Pathway that is formed as you tread the path itself. This is the Pathway of Individuation. As you assimilate the teachings of the Activation Sequence, you may begin to have a taste of this Pathway opening up inside your DNA. It will continue to open as you follow the Golden Path onwards into the Venus Sequence and the Pearl, both of which criss-cross this central column. By the time your contemplation has travelled the whole length of the Golden Path, this Pathway of Individuation will be significantly widened in your consciousness. The whole purpose of these teachings is to bring you into a stage of individuation, that beautiful yet simple place of inner equilibrium and deep calm.

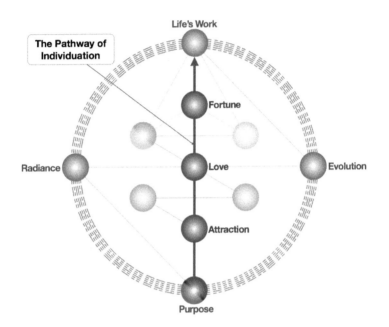

FINAL WORD

Guiding Others Along The Golden Path

As you are no doubt realising, the Golden Path is designed as a path of Self Illumination. Its true power lies in the fact that it is triggered inside you through the consistency of your own contemplation. Having said this, the Golden Path also lends itself to all kinds of approaches. You may already feel an urge to guide others through their own Activation Sequence, or indeed any of the sequences that make up the Golden Path. It is always a noble thing to want to help others in such a way. My only wish as the first journeyman of this wisdom is that you first of all travel the entire Golden Path yourself before you attempt to guide others.

The real secret to these teachings is patience and time. 2 years of contemplating the Golden Path is a minimum requirement for anyone wishing to be a guide for others. The deeper you allow the wisdom to penetrate your cells, your relationships and the fabric of your everyday life, the more you will sing out with its truth. So please be patient and take your time. Study the rich additional resources that come with the online version of the Program - its many audios, videos and webinars. There are insights and breakthroughs throughout this program that will greatly enhance your ability to understand and guide others. The Gene Keys are first and foremost a teaching about embodiment, so please consider this if you feel the urge to one day be an ambassador of the Gene Keys.

The Golden Path is also a communal knowledge that can be at its most powerful when contemplated in a group. To move through each Sphere and Pathway in your own life and at the same time to do this within a group, is a very powerful experience. When you come to contemplate the teachings of Part 3 of the Golden Path - the Pearl - you will learn about the power of communal awakening. The support of a group will affirm your own process of self illumination and quicken your breakthroughs. However you decide to tread your own Golden Path, I wish you well on your continued journey.

THE GENE KEYS
GOLDEN PATH
LOVE
A guide to your Venus Sequence

A PERSONAL INVITATION FROM RICHARD RUDD

Now that your contemplation has begun to open up an understanding of your Hologenetic Profile, you are invited to dive much deeper, by doing Part 2 of this Program, the Venus Sequence. The Venus Sequence is a longer and more extensive contemplation whose primary purpose is to soften the area around your heart, opening you up to new and undreamed of possibilities both in your personal and working life.

The Venus Sequence is one of the most challenging and uplifting aspects of working with the Gene Keys. It takes valour and patience to breathe life back into our heart, but the rewards are truly extraordinary, as those who have gone before will testify. I'd like to therefore encourage you to stand out from the crowd and take the bold leap into this deeper heart-work. You have my personal word that it is one of the most powerful revelations you will ever come across, and it will have far-reaching implications in all your relationships.

I wish you love and blessings on your continuing journey...

Richard Rudd

CPSIA information can be obtained
at www.ICGtesting.com
Printed in the USA
BVHW020243230122
626868BV00005B/279